Are You PSYCHIC?

The Official Guide for Kids

Helaine Becker

Illustrations by
Claudia Dávila

MAPLE
TREE
PRESS

Maple Tree Press Inc.
51 Front Street East, Suite 200, Toronto, Ontario M5E 1B3
www.mapletreepress.com

Distributed in Canada by Raincoast Books
9050 Shaughnessy Street, Vancouver, British Columbia V6P 6E5

Distributed in the United States by Publishers Group West
1700 Fourth Street, Berkeley, California 94710

Dedication
For Andrew, Michael, and Karl

Cataloguing in Publication Data
Becker, Helaine, 1961–
Are you psychic? : the official guide for kids / Helaine
Becker ; Claudia Dávila, illustrator.

ISBN 1-897066-20-1 (bound).   ISBN 1-897066-21-X (pbk.)

1. Psychic ability—Juvenile literature. I. Dávila, Claudia II. Title.

BF1045.C45B42 2005   j133.8   C2004-905589-5

Design & art direction: Leah Gryfe
Illustrations: Claudia Dávila

We acknowledge the financial support of the Canada Council for the Arts, the Ontario Arts
Council, the Government of Canada through the Book Publishing Industry Development
Program (BPIDP), and the Government of Ontario through the Ontario Media Development
Corporation's Book Initiative for our publishing activities.

ONTARIO ARTS COUNCIL
CONSEIL DES ARTS DE L'ONTARIO

The activities in this book have been tested and are safe when conducted as instructed.
The author and publisher accept no responsibility for any damage caused
or sustained by the use or misuse of ideas or material featured in *Are You Psychic?*

Printed in Hong Kong

A B C D E F

Contents

Are You Psychic?

You are sitting at home when all of a sudden the image of a friend pops into your mind. A few minutes later, the phone rings. Surprise! It's that very same friend calling! Coincidence or *premonition*?

You dream about a relative being ill. The following week, your family gets E-mail telling you that Auntie Jane has had a fall. Coincidence or *clairvoyance*?

You suddenly know that your math teacher is going to spring a pop quiz. You study and snag an A⁻ while everyone else gets "Unprepared." Coincidence or *telepathy*?

Have these kinds of freaky things ever happened to you? More than 67% of people say they have had experiences like these. Some people have them so often that they say they must be psychic.

Is there really such a thing as a psychic? Or is it just hocus-pocus? Since before recorded history, people all over the world have believed in psychic powers: from shamans communicating with the spirit world and with people far away to oracles predicting the future. Dreams were used to foresee the future and determine people's paths in life.

In the pages that follow, you will find out how seriously people viewed psychic powers in the past. You will meet psychics and mystics who have wowed witnesses with bang-on predictions. You will uncover some tricks used by dishonest fortune-tellers. And you will learn about scientific experiments designed to test whether or not psychic abilities are real.

With the tools in this book, you can become an investigator of psychic phenomena yourself! You will be able to set up your own experiments to find out whether or not you or your friends have psychic powers. By looking at the evidence and weighing the facts, you will be able to ponder the question, "Is there such a thing as ESP?"

Making Sense of It

People normally have five senses: taste, sight, smell, hearing, and touch. Psychics claim they have a *sixth sense*. It helps them pick up information that the rest of us miss. The sixth sense is sometimes called *extra sensory perception (ESP)*, or *second sight*. Another common name is *Psi* (pronounced *sigh*), the 23rd letter of the Greek alphabet.

It's a Mystery

The term *psychic* comes from a Greek word meaning "soul" or "mind." It refers to mysterious forces or events that cannot be explained by science. People who describe themselves as psychics claim to be extra sensitive to these forces.

Do you foresee fun and adventure in your future? If the answer is yes, turn the page.

CHAPTER 1

Mind Reading

Does your best friend often seem to know exactly what you are thinking? And how does your mom always know when you didn't brush your teeth? Can they read your mind? Here's an even spookier thought: Can *you* read *theirs*?

Mind reading is one of the most common types of ESP. It is sometimes called mental telepathy. The word mental means "mind." The word telepathy comes from the Greek words for "distant" (*tele*) and "feeling" (*pathe*). So mental telepathy is "distant-mind-feeling"—the mind-to-mind communication of thoughts, images, and emotions.

Out of this World?

In 1971, an astronaut aboard *Apollo 14* conducted his own mind-reading experiment. He sent a random series of numbers mentally to four people on Earth, 240,000 kilometres (150,000 miles) below. After the space voyage, the astronaut reported that two of the four receivers scored far better than could be explained by simple luck or coincidence.

Unusual Studies

A *parapsychologist* (pah-rah-sy-KOL-oh-jist) is a person who studies unusual and unexplained events that may or may not be supernatural in origin.

Think About It!

Parapsychologists say:

- The best mind readers are women.
- Telepathic abilities are improved by drinking cola, coffee, and tea, and by eating chocolate! (The secret ingredient is caffeine.)
- Left-handers are better mind readers than right-handers.
- Older people make better mind readers than younger ones.
- Dreams are the most common source of telepathic messages.

The idea of mind reading has been around for a long time. Australian aboriginals traditionally believe all people can do it naturally. In other tribes around the world, specially trained shamans developed and refined the skill.

In many cultures, a shaman was the focus for all psychic and spiritual activity. The shaman was a healer, storyteller, priest, and sorcerer for the tribe. He would drum, chant, or concentrate on flames to enter into a trance-like state. Then the shaman would consult with spirits to seek answers to important questions, such as where to find good hunting or how to cure an illness.

Scientists began to study mind reading seriously after World War I, doing experiments on thousands of people across Great Britain and North America. What were the results of all the experiments? As fortune-tellers at a fair might say: "The message is not clear."

Today, there is plenty of evidence that many people really can read minds. How they do it is still a mystery.

The message is not clear

Mental Magic

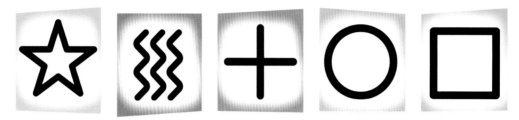

Long Distance Mind Challenge

Parapsychologist J. B. Rhine came up with a way to check ESP ability. He made a special set of 25 cards. There were five designs in all, and five cards of each design. Rhine conducted thousands of experiments, showing the cards one at a time to a "sender." The "receiver" then had to guess the correct card. Try it at home!

You'll Need

- 25 index cards
- tracing paper
- scissors
- pen, pencil, or marker
- paper to make score sheet
- two clocks
- two people: a sender and a receiver

1 Make your own deck of ESP test cards. On index cards, copy or trace five of each design shown above. Be sure all the designs are clear, but not visible through the back of the card. (This will be important when you use these cards for other activities in this book.)

2 Create a score sheet for both the sender and receiver. The sheets should look like the one on the left.

Sender's name: ―――――
Receiver's name: ―――――
Date & time: ―――――
Series #1

Sender's name: ―――――
Receiver's name: ―――――
Date & time: ―――――
Series #2

Sender's name: ―――――
Receiver's name: ―――――
Date & time: ―――――
Series #3

	Series #1	Series #2	Series #3
1	○		
2	▢		
3	〰		
4	✛		
5	▢		
6	☆		
7	✛		
8	○		
	〰		

How Did **Your Challenge** Stack Up?

Critics of Rhine's experiments said his methods were unscientific. They claimed he overlooked data that did not fit his theories. They also thought it was too easy to cheat on the tests, saying his cards were too thin, and that Rhine's test receivers (who were in the room with the senders) could see the symbols right through them! Rhine did improve his methods. For example, he started putting senders and receivers in separate rooms, but he was never able to prove once and for all that ESP exists. To be fair, it wasn't entirely his fault. Part of the problem lies in the nature of ESP. ESP is tricky to study because it doesn't necessarily happen under laboratory conditions.

3 Choose a quiet place for your test. Agree on a time to start the experiment. Have the sender move to another room with one of the clocks.

4 At the appointed time, the sender should pick up the first card of the deck and concentrate on the image. The receiver should relax and let the image appear in her mind. She writes down her guess on the score sheet. Before moving to the next card, the sender should note on a score sheet which card he was focusing on.

5 Repeat at two-minute intervals until the deck has been run through.

6 Over time, run through all 25 cards two more times. You can do this on different days.

7 Score the test by comparing the sender's and receiver's score sheets and adding up the total number of "hits" for all three series.

8 Check your score at right. Scores much lower or higher than predicted by chance may mean you have ESP!

TOTAL FOR THREE TRIALS

SCORE	ODDS	YOUR MENTAL ABILITIES
9 or less	20:1	Cool! Reverse telepathy. This might mean you are using strong mental abilities to block the correct answer.
15	even	As predicted by chance.
18	10:1	Maybe...
21	30:1	Impressive.
24	125:1	Woweee!
27	400:1	Bet you already know what we're thinking!

Picture Perfect Pair

Most people who report ESP say that it doesn't occur on demand. Instead, it shows up like a "bolt out of the blue." During the 1930s, a famous author named Upton Sinclair did a series of over a hundred experiments to see if his wife, Mary, could read his mind. He would draw a simple picture and then mentally "send" her the image. Mary drew the picture that came into her mind. The results were impressive, and caught the attention of the public.

Think About It!

- ESP seems to occur most often when something serious or startling is happening. You may all of a sudden "know" that your best friend is in trouble. But you may never guess correctly for something a little more ho-hum, like what color socks she's wearing.
- Mind reading is most common between closely related people, like married couples, twins, or siblings.
- Psychic powers weaken when people are bored, tense, tired, or distracted.

ZZZZZZZZz

Doodle Magic

Try sending pictures to a friend the way the Sinclairs did. Here's how:

You'll Need
- two pencils
- two pads of paper
- two clocks

1 Go into separate rooms where you cannot see or hear each other.

2 At an agreed-upon time, draw a simple image. You may choose one of the pictures shown here, or use one of your own creation. Don't let your friend—the receiver—know what picture you are using.

3 You should concentrate on both what the picture looks like, and how you feel when drawing it.

4 In the next room, the receiver relaxes, allowing an image to float into his mind. When the receiver thinks he has a good idea of the chosen picture, he draws it on the pad.

5 Do two or three tests before comparing the sent images with the received images.

6 Compare the pictures. How similar are they?

7 Have someone who does not know what you were testing compare the pictures. Would he say the pictures are as similar as two peas in a pod, or as different as chalk and cheese?

8 Now switch who draws and who receives. Is one of you a more effective sender or receiver?

ESP and Intuition

Have you ever had a gut feeling or a hunch? If so, then you have had an intuition. It's the feeling you get when you suddenly "know" something, but you can't quite put your finger on *how* you know. Many people believe that mind reading and ESP are kinds of intuition.

If ESP is intuition, then you probably do have some psychic talent—children and teenagers get the most hunches. More women than men report having intuition. And so do more people in the creative arts than in other fields.

But what exactly is intuition? According to the experts, it is one of the natural ways your brain works. Your sense organs collect zillions of bits of information all the time. There's so much data coming in that you can't keep track of everything. If you did, you would overload, short circuit, fry your brain! So you only pay attention to what seems important *now*, like the streetlight that has just turned red.

Even though you may not realize it, you are still picking up a ton of info. You're a walking antenna, and everything you see, hear, and feel goes into your brain's command unit.

For example, your friend is daydreamy and distracted, and chewing on her hair. Her pencil is bitten-up and her notebooks have folded bits of paper stuck between the pages. At first, these clues didn't mean anything to you. You hardly noticed them. But hours, or even days, later when you're just zoning out, all of the little details come together in your mind and—*ping!* You suddenly realize that your best friend has a secret admirer. You can't say how you know this—you don't consciously remember the chomped pencil or the secret notes. But you are sure something is going on—and as it turns out, you're right!

Think About It!

People who act on their hunches discover that their instincts grow stronger and more reliable over time. So the next time you are taking a test, if you have a gut feeling that the answer is A, go for it! Of course, that doesn't get you off the hook from studying for your next test.

Growing Your Intuition

People can "grow" their sense of intuition. In fact, many psychics recommend beefing up intuition to increase your powers of ESP.

The best way to stimulate awareness and increase your powers of intuition is to quiet your mind and free up your imagination. Try the following games to boost your observation skills and "grow" your own intuition.

Right Now Challenge

You'll Need
• your five (or six) senses

1 Take a minute and notice what you are aware of *right now*. How many things can you:
>   *See right now?*
>   *Feel right now?*
>   *Hear right now?*
>   *Smell right now?*
>   *Taste right now?*

2 Do this activity whenever you think of it to pump up your awareness of your environment.

I Spy with My Little Eye Game

You'll Need
• an illustrated children's book

1 Find a quiet place where you can sit undisturbed.

2 Study the illustrations in the picture book. Notice as many details as you can on each page.

3 When you have finished, go back to the beginning. See if you can find one more detail on each page that you did not notice during your first reading.

The Parrot Challenge

You'll Need
- a friend
- a book

1 Have your friend read two or three lines from the book to you.

2 Repeat back *word for word* what you heard. How accurate were you?

3 Gradually increase the number of lines.

4 Take turns parroting each other. By sharpening your listening skills, you will become more aware of what others are really saying.

remember the words

repeat after me

one more time to get it right

Liar, Liar, Pants on Fire!

You'll Need
- a friend

1 Have your friend tell you about something true that happened to him during the day. Watch his face and body language carefully.

2 Next, have your friend lie to you about something that didn't really happen during the day. Again, watch his face and body language.

3 Can you see any differences when he is telling the truth and when he is lying? Let your friend test you.

4 Now, mixing up the order of true and false statements, tell each other several truths and lies. Can you tell when he is lying? What else do your friend's expressions or gestures tell you about his mood or thoughts?

5 Watch other people carefully when they are speaking. What can you learn about them just by quietly observing?

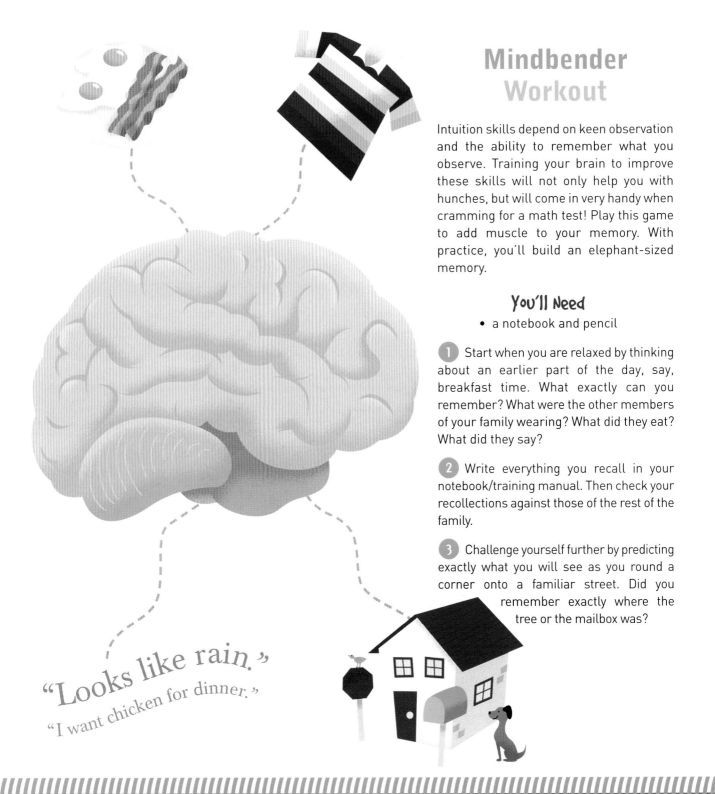

Mindbender Workout

Intuition skills depend on keen observation and the ability to remember what you observe. Training your brain to improve these skills will not only help you with hunches, but will come in very handy when cramming for a math test! Play this game to add muscle to your memory. With practice, you'll build an elephant-sized memory.

You'll Need
- a notebook and pencil

1 Start when you are relaxed by thinking about an earlier part of the day, say, breakfast time. What exactly can you remember? What were the other members of your family wearing? What did they eat? What did they say?

2 Write everything you recall in your notebook/training manual. Then check your recollections against those of the rest of the family.

3 Challenge yourself further by predicting exactly what you will see as you round a corner onto a familiar street. Did you remember exactly where the tree or the mailbox was?

"Looks like rain."

"I want chicken for dinner."

In the Zzzzzone Quest

You're most likely to experience ESP when your mind is quiet and relaxed—like when you are just falling asleep. As you drift off to the Land of Nod, your brain begins to produce more *alpha waves*. Alpha waves indicate a state of wakeful sleep or deep relaxation. You may see images or swirling colors in your mind's eye. This is often when psychic impressions appear.

Snoozing may be a great way to tune in to ESP reception, but it's a little impractical in the middle of class. For times when you need to be alert, you can keep your antennae tweaked with a little meditation. Many people also use meditation to boost their energy and improve their concentration. Here's how to do it:

You'll Need
- a comfortable, quiet place where you will not be disturbed

1 Get comfy. Be prepared to stay in the same position for about ten minutes.

2 Close your eyes. Concentrate on your breathing as you inhale and exhale.

3 Try not to think about anything. When an idea or thought comes to mind just "observe" it, then let it go. Return to concentrating on your breathing.

4 After ten minutes, open your eyes. Stretch. You have meditated!

5 Practice this activity whenever you feel like you need quiet time, and before doing the challenges in this book.

Transcendental Meditation

Experienced meditators can also go into a trance, which is really an "awake/asleep" state. In this state, people's minds are more open to new ideas and impressions. It is also considered an ideal state for receiving telepathic messages.

Think About It!

The most successful psychics are excellent observers. They have trained their senses to work at an unusually high level. They pay attention to details. Do you think this might also be true of the best scientists?

What Do You Think?

In this chapter, you have uncovered a little about ancient beliefs in mental telepathy. You have also duplicated scientific experiments designed to prove the existence of mental telepathy, and explored the relationship between ESP and intuition. With what you now know, do you believe that mental telepathy is real? Or do you doubt it exists? Perhaps what you learn in the next chapter will help you decide.

CHAPTER 2

Fakes & Phonies

A lot of people experience ESP, but not everyone who claims to be psychic is genuine. Given a receptive audience and a few tricks hidden up a sleeve, a "psychic" stage performer can be very convincing indeed. So can a con artist who persuades you that she will solve all of your problems—for a fee. Fakes can make you believe that they have the power to read your mind.

How telepathic are lies and deception? Not very, but that's how some phony psychics work their "magic." In this chapter you'll find out how to fine-tune your phony detectors to spot the frauds and fakers making false claims.

Getting Warmer . . .

Most honest people would never suspect that a psychic would stoop to spying. But a technique called *warm reading* is really just a warm and fuzzy term for snooping.

When dishonest psychic readers or fortune-tellers need to show that they know something unique about you, they may use the services of assistants or private investigators to sniff out vital info. Using this kind of preparation, a psychic mysteriously "knows" facts about you, such as when and where you were born, or the name of your parents or other relatives. Most of this stuff is easy to find out. Given a little advance warning, a psychic can dig up all kinds of "confidential information."

Many professional psychics travel with an assistant. Their job is to find out about the community for warm readings. Some show-biz psychics may even pay local informants to get the goods on people coming to the show. Sometimes they plant assistants in the audience to make their act more convincing.

A Gruesome Twosome

In the 1920s, a traveling mind-reading duo called the Cornells claimed to have had a vision of a murder. The Chicago police dragged the river, and sure enough, they found a body exactly as the Cornells predicted. It was later discovered that the Cornells had bought the body from a mortuary and had thrown it into the river at the "predicted" spot.

Getting Really Warm!

In 1975, psychic David Bubar predicted that there would be a fire at a Connecticut factory. He was later convicted for setting the fire that he had "foreseen" several weeks earlier!

Think About It!

Some fakes can be harmless or entertaining, but those who prey on victims with serious problems are cruel—even criminal. For instance, a phony claiming to "know" where a missing person is can waste valuable time sending police investigators on a wild goose chase, and give false hope to someone who is desperate.

Are your phony detectors tingling? Test them out in the pages ahead.

Going Fishing

Fishing is another technique used by phony psychics. When a psychic fishes, he or she asks very vague questions and then gets you to supply the answers. The phony uses the clues you provide to fool you into thinking he or she knows something special.

Here is an example of fishing, below. Can you see exactly where the fortune-teller has fished?

Most people do not realize they have been fished. Why not? There are a few reasons. One is *wishful thinking*. Anyone who visits a psychic hopes something extraordinary will happen. In this case, wishing will make it true—people will believe what they want to believe.

Another possible reason is *selective thinking*. Scientific studies have shown that people routinely forget the occasions when a psychic has goofed. They remember the hits and not the misses. It may be because our brains focus on interesting and unusual events. Think about how you can sleep through a familiar sound, but wake with a start when you hear something unfamiliar. In the same way, you may tune out the ordinary, wrong guesses (boring), and tune in when the psychic makes an unexpected, accurate comment (cool!).

A fisher will also watch you carefully, looking for non-verbal clues that tell him if he is on the right track. He will change his comments depending on your feedback. In this way, he'll be sure to tell you exactly what you want to hear.

Reeling You In

A good fisher still needs to know where to fish. This is why experienced "mind readers" stock up on useful information. For example, professional mind reader Ian Rowland says he has committed to memory:

- the most common male and female names given to newborns in different years.
- lists of items likely to be lying around the house such as old calendars, photo albums, newspaper clippings, etc.
- the most common topics on people's minds: love, money, career, health, and travel.
- the news of the day.

Think About It!

Scientists have found that the muscles in our bodies not only reflect our feelings, but also help create them. Since you smile when you feel happy, your brain will assume that you *are* happy if your muscles take the shape of a smile. Psychics who mimic their clients' facial expressions, consciously or unconsciously, might find this effect working during a reading. If you are tense, the psychic who copies your expression may begin to feel tense too! He can then honestly report that he is getting a feeling of tension from you.

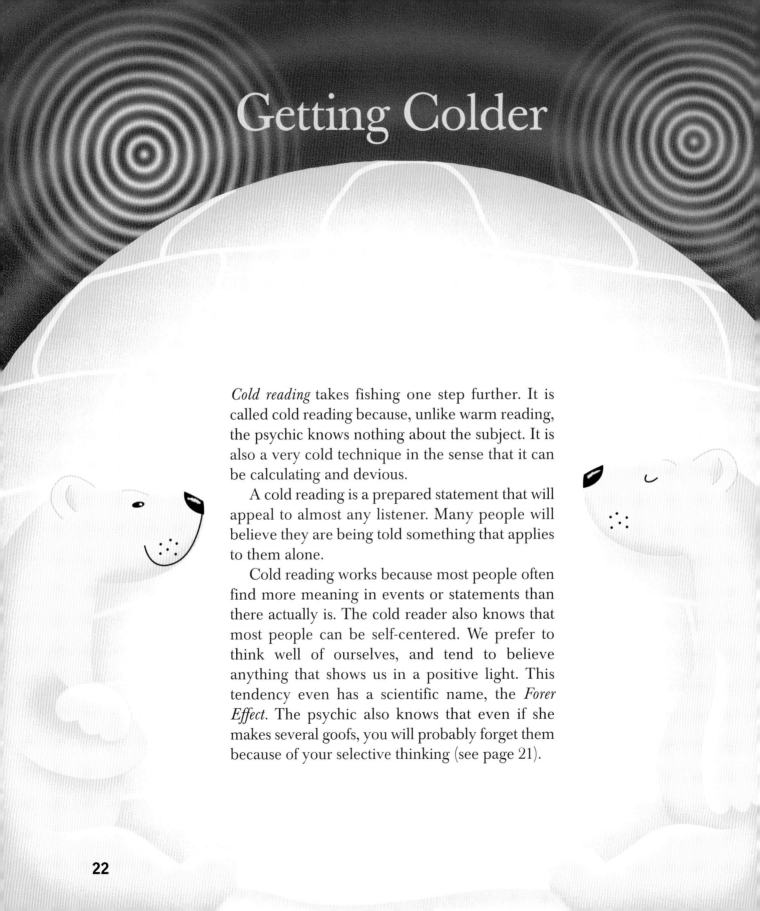

Getting Colder

Cold reading takes fishing one step further. It is called cold reading because, unlike warm reading, the psychic knows nothing about the subject. It is also a very cold technique in the sense that it can be calculating and devious.

A cold reading is a prepared statement that will appeal to almost any listener. Many people will believe they are being told something that applies to them alone.

Cold reading works because most people often find more meaning in events or statements than there actually is. The cold reader also knows that most people can be self-centered. We prefer to think well of ourselves, and tend to believe anything that shows us in a positive light. This tendency even has a scientific name, the *Forer Effect*. The psychic also knows that even if she makes several goofs, you will probably forget them because of your selective thinking (see page 21).

Feeling Chilled?

This is based on an actual cold reading used by a professional mentalist. Does it describe you?

Some of your dreams for the future can be pretty unrealistic. At times you can be outgoing. You enjoy parties and get along well with others. At other times, however, you feel shy and prefer to keep to yourself. You are an independent thinker, but also enjoy belonging to a group. You prefer a certain amount of change and variety, and become bored and frustrated when parents or teachers restrict your actions. At times you wonder if you are making good decisions in your life. You may seem calm on the outside, but tend to be insecure and worried on the inside. While you have some weaknesses, you can usually make up for them. You have a great deal of unused ability that you have not yet turned to your advantage.

North Pole Challenge

Cold readings can be fun to perform! Begin by making a list of general statements that are true for most people. For example, say that they work hard to improve themselves, want to fit in, care about people, can be shy or outgoing at different times. Add some specific comments that may not apply to everyone. The more "facts" you supply, the more likely you will be to have hits. This technique—throwing out as much as possible to see what sticks—is called *shotgunning*. If your facts don't fit perfectly, don't worry. Thanks to selective thinking (see page 21), your subject will probably forget any bloopers. Tell people what they want to hear—positive statements about their good qualities. Always be kind. Do not insult your subject.

You'll Need
- a subject
- a pen and paper or computer if you intend to write and/or memorize your text.

1 Prepare your speech, then set the stage. A few days ahead, tell your subjects that you have discovered that you are psychic. You sometimes "know" things about other people.

2 Refuse to do any reading for several days. Act mysterious, aloof, and a bit uncomfortable with your "skill."

3 When you believe your subjects are convinced of your sincerity, choose one person whom you do not know very well and who does not know you.

4 Take their palm in your hand and hold it for a few moments with your eyes closed. Open your eyes, and stare deeply into theirs.

5 Recite your memorized cold reading.

6 While giving the reading, observe your subject carefully. Listen to what she says, but also watch her body language, breathing, and eye movements. Adjust what you say based on these reactions.

7 Listen in amazement to the gasps of surprise!

Faking It

Maybe you can read minds, or maybe you can't. Until you know for sure, you can have fun using these tricks taken from the repertoire of famous stage magicians. Maybe you can even convince your friends that you really are psychic.

Coin Toss Up

You'll Need

- an envelope
- an index card
- a pencil
- a nickel
- a quarter
- a dime
- a small white sticker, or a piece of paper and a small piece of tape
- an audience of at least one person

1. Before your audience arrives, write this on the front of the envelope: "You will choose the nickel."

2. On the index card, write: "You will choose the dime." Place the index card inside the envelope.

3. On the small paper or sticker, write: "I knew you would choose the quarter." Stick the note to the tail side of the quarter (so it's not visible when the quarter is tails down).

4. Put all the change in the envelope. The coin heads should all be facing toward the back of the envelope so they'll slide out heads up.

5. Now you are ready for your audience. Make sure to keep the front of the envelope—the side with the writing on it—hidden from them.

6. Open the flap and gently slide the coins onto a table.

7. Put the envelope, facedown, off to the side. Keep the envelope closed so no one can see the index card inside!

8. Tell a friend that you can read her mind. Ask her to point to one coin from the three on the table.

After she does, ask if she wants to change her mind. It doesn't matter if she changes her mind at all, just make sure she knows that she is free to do so.

9. When your friend has made her choice, do the following:
- *If she has chosen the quarter*, ask her to turn all the coins over. She will find your prediction stuck to the back of the quarter!

- *If she has chosen the dime*, open the envelope and take out the index card. Remember, this card says, "You will choose the dime." Quickly show that there are no other cards in the envelope.

- *If she has chosen the nickel*, turn over the envelope. Your prediction, "You will choose the nickel" is written on the front!

10. While your friend is still in shock, quickly scoop up the coins, slip them into the envelope, and put it in your pocket.

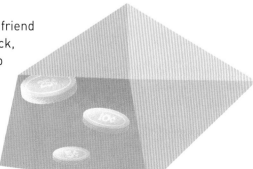

Color Magic

You'll Need
- a box of crayons
- an audience of at least two people

1. Holding your hands behind you, turn your back to the audience. Tell your subject to choose one crayon from the box you have provided. While he's choosing, explain that you will be able to sense what color crayon is chosen, because of your amazing psychic abilities.

2. When your subject has selected a crayon, have him place it in your hand without you seeing it, and hide the remaining crayons so they are out of your sight.

3. Turn to your audience, keeping the crayon behind your back.

4. Hold the crayon behind you in one hand. Using a fingernail of your free hand, scrape some wax from the crayon.

5. Still holding the crayon behind your back, bring the free hand forward. As you do, discreetly look at your nail to see what color you have scraped from the crayon.

6. When you are sure of the crayon's color, announce it to your spellbound audience. Then show the crayon. Ta-dah!

7. While your audience applauds, gently scrape your fingernail clean with the fingers of the same hand. Use the other hand to return the crayon.

What Do You Think?

In this chapter, you have uncovered some of the ways that phonies fake psychic ability. You even played some mind-reading tricks of your own. Do you think all psychics are phony-baloney? Or are there genuine psychics out there too? Maybe the next chapter will help you "see" this issue more clearly. Read on....

CHAPTER 3

Clairvoyance

Clairvoyance is a second type of ESP. The term comes from the French words that mean "clear sight." Clairvoyance is different from mental telepathy in one main way. Clairvoyants say they can see far-away objects, events, or places without another person's help. They call their gift second sight.

There have been many scientific experiments done on clairvoyance. The most famous were performed at the Stanford Research Institute in California. The experiments began in 1973 and ran for over 20 years. The U.S. Central Intelligence Agency (CIA) used the tests to see if clairvoyants could spy on the Soviet military, without leaving California! Though the CIA engineer who managed the project reported that they "produced some amazing descriptions," overall the results were not considered a great success.

Some people who claim to be clairvoyants say they first realized it when they saw *auras*. Young children frequently say they see colors, shadows, or wavy, flickering lights around people's bodies, which sound a lot like typical reports of auras. They are amazed when they realize that other people cannot see them too.

Are auras real? Some psychics believe that everyone produces a vibrating energy field and that the field is an extension of the body, surrounding it like an envelope. This is the aura. They say the outer edge of the aura is your body's true boundary, not your skin. Scientists agree that there is a vibrating energy field around the body—all living creatures do give off electromagnetic radiation. This may, in fact, be the aura you can see or feel.

Good Vibrations

In everyday speech, people sometimes refer to the aura as *vibes*, a short form of the word "vibrations."

How Aura You Feeling?

Psychics say that aura colors can change from day to day and reflect your moods and situations, as well as your general nature. Look below to see what the aura colors might mean.

The Meaning of Aura Colors

Deep Red: This person will be physically active, hardworking, and action-oriented, with lots of strength and stamina.

Red: This aura indicates excitement, energy, and a love of competition. A person with a red aura is a natural leader, innovator, and promoter.

Orange: These positive, adventurous people enjoy life and love challenges and thrills. Expect them to be exciting, productive, and successful at school and work.

Yellow-Brown: People with this aura tend to be analytical, intellectual, and detail oriented. They prefer structure and security. Their love of logic and precision makes them excellent scientists.

Yellow: People with this aura are playful, sunny, creative, and fun to be around. They are generous, easy-going, and warm-hearted.

Green: The "teacher" aura. This color signifies a very social person who loves to communicate and is an excellent host or hostess.

Deep Green: Deep green auras signal responsible people with quick minds. These ambitious folks tend to be goal-oriented and good organizers.

Blue: People with blue auras tend to be compassionate, sensitive, and loving. They frequently have a desire to help others and to be of service.

Indigo: Many people with this aura are artists. They care about feelings, and bring a sense of calm and clarity to encounters with others.

Violet: Violet auras reflect an innovative nature. People with this aura tend to be intuitive, artistic, and idealistic. The "marching to your own drummer" aura!

Lavender: Daydreamers frequently have lavender auras. These imaginative people often seem gentle and fragile, but they possess inner strength.

White: The "healer's" aura. A white aura signals a very spiritual personality.

"Feelin' the Vibes" Challenge

Not very many people *see* auras. But you can *feel* them much more easily. Try this:

You'll Need
• your two hands

1 Hold your hands in front of you at shoulder height, palms facing each other. Your palms should be about 15 cm (6 in.) apart. Count to 30.

2 Slowly bring your palms together. Before your hands actually touch, you should begin to feel the air between them grow thicker, spongier, and more resistant. It might even begin to feel warm. Your fingertips might tingle. This is supposedly your aura.

3 When you are certain you can feel the aura, gradually move your palms farther and farther away. See how far apart you can bring your hands before you lose the feeling of the aura.

The "Do You See It Aura Not?" Challenge

You'll Need
• a friend

1 Ask a friend to stand against a plain wall.

2 Half close your eyes. Relax them so that when you look at your friend (for about ten seconds), she looks slightly blurry.

3 Now look slightly off to the side. Your friend should just be visible in the corner of your eye. Can you see a vague outline in the shape of her body? How thick is it? How bright is it? What color is it?

Think About It!

Was the tingling in your fingertips caused by an aura, or is there another explanation? Might it have been because you were holding your hands up above your heart, and the blood was draining out of them? Repeat the Vibes challenge just holding up one hand. Do you feel the same tingling sensation in your fingers?

Heart of Hearts

If you stare at a dark image against a contrasting background, your eyes will retain a picture of the image, even after you look away. Try it by staring at the pink heart for 30 seconds. Then look at a plain, light-colored wall. Do you see a floating green heart? This is called the after-image. The auras people report seeing may simply be an after-image of their friends' bodies. Most reports of auras describe colors in the pink or green range — colors that are consistent with typical after-images.

How's Your Aura?

People say your aura mirrors and projects your personality and moods. It ebbs and flows as you go through your daily life. It changes with your energy level. It reflects your inner world.

In theory, then, your aura can affect people around you. A person with a negative aura (someone who is angry or depressed) can make other people feel rotten. Think about the expression, "Something made the hairs on the back of my neck stand up." Could the speaker be responding to a negative aura? On the other hand, a person with a positive, vibrant aura can make you feel good. These people are the ones that everyone wants to be near.

When you are with a friend, ask yourself some questions. How does being with this person make me feel? Do I feel calm and relaxed? Happy and excited? Tense or on edge? Test your reactions to some other friends. Do some people, for no reason at all, make you feel terrific? Do others make you feel nervous, even scared or sad? What can you sense about people with your eyes closed? In a room full of activity, can you tell when someone has just walked into the room or has just left? Can you tell who they are?

The Good Vibrations Challenge

Maybe you have never seen an aura. But that doesn't mean it isn't there, right? Next time you're hanging out with a friend, try this experiment. It uses an ordinary metal hanger to detect your friend's aura.

You'll Need
- an ordinary metal hanger
- a friend

1 Facing each other, stand about 3 m (10 ft.) away from your friend.

2 Hold a hanger vertically in your hand with the hook pointing at your friend. Lightly clasp the straight bar of the hanger so that it remains vertical, but can swivel in your hand.

3 Ask your friend to concentrate all of his energy on the hanger. He should try to make the hanger swing.

4 Have your friend slowly move toward you, still concentrating on the hanger. At some point, long before he can touch the hanger, you may feel it start to move from side to side.

5 See if your friend can move the hanger more by extending his arms toward you, or by stepping backward or forward, or from side to side. With practice, he may be able to move the hanger in your hand from clear across the room!

6 Are you actually dowsing (see right) when you do this aura search? Believers say that the hanger is picking up electrostatic and electromagnetic waves from the object. Others say dowsing works because of unconscious movements by the person holding the hanger, in which muscle contractions force the rod to move without their knowledge.

Dowsing Rods

Traditionally, people practiced the art of *dowsing* to find water or precious minerals in the earth. This technique was widely used well into the nineteenth century. The dowser would use a forked branch that would bob or move on its own when the substance he was searching for was nearby. A coat hanger can also be used to dowse. In modern times, dowsing has been used by soldiers to locate buried mines in Vietnam, by archeologists to dig for treasures, and by oil companies to find oil deposits. Some doctors in the past even used rod-like devices to pinpoint the source of their patients' complaints.

Think About It!

Many traditional cultures believe in the *evil eye*. People who "possess" the evil eye, it is thought, can influence others, causing bad fortune or sickness. A modern psychic might say that the evil eye is a person with a negative aura. Skeptics say that "victims" of the "evil eye" are responding to the power of suggestion (see page 52).

Second Sight Spree

Seeing auras is one thing. Second sight is another. What can you see with your mental telescope? Find out with the activities on these pages.

Second-Sight Challenge

Can you catch a glimpse of life in Lhasa, or goings-on in Gambia? The best way to find out is to take this second-sight challenge.

You'll Need
- The ESP cards that you made in chapter 1 (see page 8)
- recording sheets and markers
- table

You can do this experiment on your own or with a friend.

1 Shuffle the ESP cards and place them facedown on the table.

2 Choose a card, but don't flip it over.

3 Without anyone looking at the card, record your guess of what is on the card on your paper.

4 Repeat for all of the cards in the deck.

5 After finishing the run, check the cards against your answers, and keep track of how many hits (correct answers) you had.

6 Shuffle and repeat several more runs, until you become tired or bored.

7 Refer to the scoring chart on page 9 to check your results.

Second-Sight Solitaire

No pal in sight? This is a great challenge to do on your own.

You'll Need
- a regular deck of playing cards

1 Remove the four aces from the deck. Place them in a row faceup in front of you.

2 Shuffle the rest of the cards.

3 Without looking, try to sense the suit of the card (heart, club, diamond, or spade) on the top of the deck. Place it facedown under the ace of the same suit.

4 Repeat until you have placed all of the cards in columns below the four aces.

5 Turn over the cards in each column.

6 Count up how many hits you got in all suits—how many spades you have in the spades column, and the same for hearts, diamonds, and clubs.

7 Check your score against the chart at right.

TOTAL PER SOLITAIRE RUN		
HITS	ODDS	SCORE
0 to 4	20:1	Possible reverse clairvoyance.
12	Even	As chance would predict.
16	10:1	Maybe...
18	20:1	Looking good!
19	100:1	Excellent!
20	400:1	Seeing really is believing!

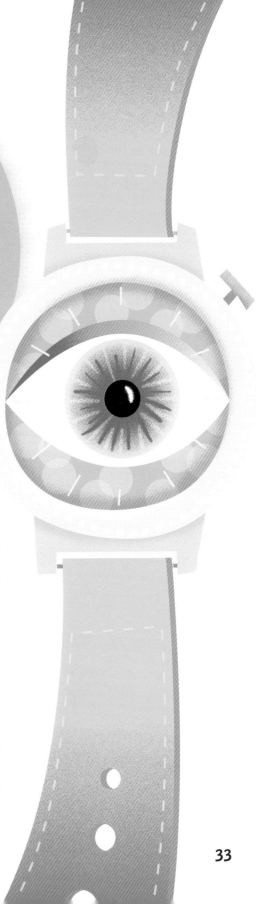

Second Sight and the **Third Eye**

Many psychics believe we possess a *third eye* in the area of our forehead, and that it is this inner eye at work in cases of clairvoyance. For thousands of years, Hindus in India have believed that within the human body there are seven major energy centers, or *chakras*. Each chakra resembles a spinning wheel or flower, and is associated with a specific color, part of the body, and ability or emotion. The sixth chakra is located in the center of the forehead. It is known as the *third eye chakra*. It is associated with vision and mental clarity. Mystics are commonly said to have a very strong sixth chakra.

Third Eye **Sight**

Some people practice a form of clairvoyance called *psychometry*. The term comes from the Greek words *psyche* (soul) and *metre* (measurement). Psychics say they can receive clairvoyant impressions from objects such as stones, photographs, or jewelry. The psychic touches the objects, sometimes pressing them to his forehead for closer contact with the third eye. He then sees mental images having to do with the person who owns the object. Test your third eye sight with this challenge.

You'll Need
• three or four watches belonging to friends

1 Close your eyes and have a friend give you one of the watches.

2 Hold the watch and bring it close to your forehead, to make closer contact with your third eye.

3 Do any images connected with any of your friends come to mind? Without feeling for any telltale characteristics, can you guess whose watch you are holding?

Sight Challenges

Clairvoyants see visions—pictures in their minds of objects that are not really there. They sometimes use techniques like the ones here to develop their own abilities.

Seeing Things?

With a little practice, you can develop the power to conjure simple visions with your eyes open! Try it and *see* for yourself.

You'll Need
- colored paper
- colored markers
- glue stick and scissors

1 Make yourself four cards, using the four designs pictured below.

2 Settle yourself comfortably in a brightly lit room. Choose one of the four designs. Place it in front of you on a tabletop, and look at the design for three minutes.

3 Close your eyes. You will see the after-image of the picture in your mind's eye, in contrasting colors. For example, you will see a blue triangle on a yellow background, or a pink square on a white background. Continue to observe the after-image with your eyes closed.

4 Repeat the procedure with the other three designs.

5 Follow the steps above at least once a day for three or four days. You may notice after practicing this activity that you can close your eyes at any time and clearly envision the four images.

6 Practice seeing the images for several more days, without using the actual pictures as prompts.

7 When you feel like you can picture any of these images clearly and at will, choose one, and picture it in your mind's eye. Then open your eyes. The image should remain, hanging in space in front of you!

Vision **Quests**

In North America, many First Nations people held *vision quests*, rituals in which people would seek help from the spirits. Usually, the person was a girl or a boy about to go through puberty. The seeker would go to a sacred place in the wilderness and meditate for several days without food or water, hoping to induce a clairvoyant vision. The vision would then guide the person or provide luck in war, love, or childbirth. It was believed that a person who had endured the hardship of a vision quest would emerge strengthened and with a new sense of purpose.

You've Got **Mail**

You'll Need

- a friend
- notepad and pen or pencil
- six pictures from old magazines that you have permission to cut up
- six identical envelopes, large enough to hold one picture

1 Have your friend tear out pictures from an old magazine, without showing you what they are.

2 Your friend should then place one picture in each envelope. If the images show through, tell her to wrap each picture first in a sheet of white paper.

3 Shuffle the envelopes so that neither of you knows which picture is inside, then number the envelopes from one to six.

4 Relax in a quiet, dim room. Mark the first sheet of your notepad "Envelope 1." Pressing the envelope to your forehead, allow an image to form in your mind.

5 Record the image you saw in words or pictures on your notepad.

6 Repeat for the five remaining envelopes. Take as much time as you need. If you become bored or tired during the experiment, take a break and return to it later.

7 After you have completed all six envelopes, open them. Compare the notes and drawings that you made with the actual pictures. Would both you and your friend consider them to be accurate?

Barnyard Psi

There are many accounts of animals having second sight. Check out these wild stories. Do you think these pets were practicing clairvoyance?

In the eighteenth century, a "learned pig" and a "wonderful intelligent goose" made waves in England. The pig "read minds" of people in the audience by picking flashcards with words printed on them. The goose "clairvoyantly" identified playing cards and secret numbers.

In 1904, a German horse named Clever Hans caused a stir with his apparent psychic abilities. That is, until a psychologist determined that questioners—including Hans' trainer—were unintentionally giving the horse clues. Hans stamped his hoof for answers to yes or no questions, or numbers. The

psychologist pointed out that Hans would only stop stamping when the observer relaxed—as soon as the correct answer had been reached!

In 1929, a "telepathic" horse named Lady Wonder stupefied audiences with her abilities. Lady was trained to operate a machine composed of levers that activated alphabet cards. Lady would press the levers with her nose to spell out answers to questions.

A magician named Milbourne Christopher visited the elderly Lady in 1956. He told Lady's trainer his name was "John Banks." When he later asked Lady, "What is my name?" the horse spelled B-A-N-K-S. Christopher suspected that Lady was responding to the trainer's "slight movement" of her training rod whenever Lady was at the lever the trainer wanted her to press.

Test Your **Own Pet**

Is your little Fluffy psychic? Find out by running this experiment.

You'll Need
- pet food
- two identical bowls
- two identical batches of your pet's food
- score sheet and marker
- your pet

1. Place equal amounts of the food in each bowl.

2. Put the bowls in an accessible place.

3. Decide which bowl you want your pet to use. Using your mental powers of concentration, send your message to your pet.

4. Record which bowl your pet ate from on your recording sheet.

5. Repeat this experiment every day for several weeks. Chance would predict that your pet will choose the "correct" bowl 50% (or half) of the time. If, over 90 days, your pet scores significantly better than this, you may have a four-pawed celebrity in your house.

Think About It!

Might you be giving sensory cues to your pet like the ones given to Clever Hans? How could you design an experiment to prevent this possibility?

What Do You Think?

In this chapter, you have delved into auras and chakras, visions, and visionaries. After trying the experiments and studying the evidence, are you convinced that clairvoyance is real? Do you still need further proof? There may be just the proof you need in the next chapter. Look into your crystal ball for a clue, or simply turn the page.

Fortune-Telling

Imagine that you are a farmer in ancient Greece. You want to know if there will be enough rain this year for you to plant your crops. What do you do? Probably, like many other Greeks of the day, you consult an *oracle*. Oracles were fortune-tellers who were thought to have divine power. They could predict the future and answer your questions. Today, many people still consult fortune-tellers to find out what the future holds.

Even more people report having had psychic experiences where they suddenly "know" something is going to happen. In fact, precognition—knowing the future—is the most commonly reported form of ESP.

People who experience precognition say they hear voices, see visions, or experience a flash of "knowing" in the mind. Precognition can be induced during trances. Many psychics use tools such as crystal balls or tarot cards to divine the future. Most often, though, the knowledge comes in dreams.

In most reported cases of precognition, a predicted event happens within 24–48 hours. The prediction often (85% of the time) involves a person close to the seer, such as a spouse, family member, or intimate friend. Most predictions involve unhappy events. There are four times more predictions of illness, accidents, or deaths than of happier events.

Think About It!

Parapsychologists believe that up to half of precognitive experiences may contain information that can help avert disasters.

Visionary Vocabulary

The term *precognition* generally refers to knowledge of a specific event before it happens. The term *premonition* is more a sense or a feeling that something unknown is about to happen. *Prediction* usually refers to the future of an individual, whereas a *prophecy* usually refers to a whole group of people such as a nation. *Divination* is the art of prediction using special tools such as pendulums, crystal balls, tarot cards, stars, numbers, or tea leaves.

Testing Precognition

No one really knows how precognition might work. Although it remains unexplained, precognition is the easiest type of ESP to test for in the laboratory. It's easy to measure the accuracy of predictions for simple events like the roll of dice or the order of cards. See for yourself by doing the challenge below based on real lab tests.

Future Quest

You'll Need
- your ESP cards from page 8
- a notepad
- pen, pencil, or marker

1 Choose a quiet, relaxed time and place for your test.

2 Shuffle the ESP cards, facedown. Place the deck facedown in front of you, without looking at the cards.

3 Predict the order of all 25 of the cards in the deck, recording your guesses on your notepad.

4 When you have completed your predictions, deal out the cards faceup one by one. Record each card on your sheet as it appears.

5 Repeat three times, running through all 25 cards, recording your guesses and the actual order.

6 To score the test, add up the total number of hits (correct answers) for all three series.

7 Check your score on the table on page 9. Scores significantly lower or higher than predicted by chance may indicate ESP potential.

Getting Ahead of Yourself

Watch out for *displacement effects* that may skew your results. A displacement effect is when you predict cards in the correct order, but they are slightly off in terms of when they appear. So for example, your prediction for the first card matches the second card, your prediction for the second card matches the third card, etc. In other words, you correctly predicted the cards, but farther ahead in time than you expected! Your score might actually be higher than you originally thought.

Think About It!

On October 21, 1966, 144 people were killed in a landslide in Wales. In three surveys that were taken after the tragedy, more than 200 people claimed to have had premonitions about the disaster. The premonitions included depression, a feeling that something bad was about to happen, impressions of billowing black clouds, and of children screaming and running. Does this prove that precognition exists? Or did people incorrectly remember the things that they had felt or thought several weeks earlier? Or perhaps people saw a connection between two unrelated events, just because they occurred close together in time.

Double, Double Toil and Trouble . . .

In Shakespeare's tragic play *Macbeth*, King Macbeth meets with three witches in the forest and asks them to predict his future. They mix up a mysterious brew in a big pot and look into it for the answer. Although Macbeth believes the witches promise him success, they actually foretell his doom. Unaware of his mistake, Macbeth seals his fate and all is lost, proving that predictions are fine as long as they are interpreted correctly.

In Your Dreams, Pal . . .

Dreams have fascinated human beings since the dawn of time. Those nightly visions that creep into our sleep have been open to interpretation and theory for as long as there have been comfortable places to curl up in.

Throughout history, people from many cultures have thought that dreams carried messages from the gods. There are hundreds of recorded instances of prophecies coming in the form of dreams.

It wasn't only in ancient times that dreams were considered worth looking into. Many studies on telepathy and precognition in dreams were done between 1962 and 1974 at the Dream Laboratory of the Maimonides Medical Center in New York. Overall, matches between the subjects' dreams and actual events were way above chance. The experiments also showed that psychic dreams tend to be unusually vivid; have exceptionally bright colors; and have a lot of detail. They also tend to be puzzling to the dreamer, and unrelated to events of the previous week or to thoughts on the dreamer's mind.

But what could it possibly mean?

Dream Along with Me

Do you have dreams that predict the future? The best way to find out is to keep a dream journal.

You'll Need
• a notebook   • pen or pencil   • yellow highlighter

1 Keep the notebook and pen near your bed. If you wake up in the middle of the night from a dream, jot down some notes about it. Date the top of every page so you will know when you dreamed each dream.

2 Every morning, when you wake up, linger in bed for a few moments. Allow your mind to drift. Try to recapture the dream you were having shortly before waking. As soon as you can recall the dream, write it down.

Truly Large

Are psychic dreams for real, or are they just coincidences? If you are a math whiz, you might say that the Law of Truly Large Numbers is what causes them. The law says that when you are working with a big enough number of people, things, or events, you're bound to find a lot of really freaky coincidences.

Let's say that the odds of dreaming about a plane crash on the night before one happens are a million to one. Sounds pretty unlikely, right? But wait. Studies show that each of us might have an average of 250 different dream themes per night. Multiply the number of possible dream themes by the number of people in the world (six billion). Then divide that figure by a million (the one in a million chance). You wind up with 15 million people who may have had a plane crash dream. So maybe your freaky dream wasn't so freaky after all.

3 Keep track of your dreams for several months. With practice, you will discover that your dream recall improves. If you have any unusual or vivid dreams, make a star in your journal beside them.

4 If you discover that any of your dreams are predictive or telepathic in nature, highlight them with a yellow highlighter. Watch for puns and word play. If you had a dream about breaking *glasses* of juice, might it be related to the accident you had later that week when you stepped on your sun*glasses*? If you think this is a bit of a stretch, remember, that *is* the way dreams work. It's also why interpretations are unreliable and often doubted!

Good Fortune or Goodbye!

Most rulers in ancient times used divination, or reading the future, in order to decide their actions. Rulers relied on prophecies made by high priests to know how to avoid natural disasters, when to engage in warfare, or whom to marry. Since an entire society's survival often depended on the accuracy of a prediction, the priest had enormous power. However, if the priest's prophecy was incorrect, the penalty was usually death.

In ancient Rome, there were special priests called *augers*. The augers saw messages from the gods in patterns in the clouds, the path of a bird's flight, smoke rising from a hearth, or the markings on animals. The priests used their psychic and spiritual powers to decipher these omens and advise the rulers. The Chinese had court astrologers who would predict the future by casting lots (early forms of dice), bones, and other objects, while the Egyptians had their priests sleep in temples, hoping that the gods would reveal information to them in their dreams.

The Delphic
Oracle

From about 1400 BC until 381 AD, the most famous oracle of all was at Delphi, a mountainous site in central Greece. People traveled from all over Europe to Delphi, where there was a temple dedicated to the god Apollo.

The oracle, who was always a woman, made her predictions from a natural chamber in the depths of the mountain. There, she would sit on a three-legged stool over vents in the rocks that gave out a sweet-smelling vapor. Breathing the fumes, the oracle would fall into a trance. In an otherworldly voice, she would then relate a message that supposedly came from the god Apollo.

Think About It!

Recent archeological and geological studies have shown that the gas coming from cracks in the rocks at Delphi contains the chemical ethylene. This gas can cause hallucinations when inhaled.

Feathered
Forecasts

Some people still believe in these predictions left over from ancient Roman times:

- Good luck will follow if birds suddenly fly across the sky from left to right.
- If you see a red bird, make a wish — it will come true.
- When birds call, count the number of cries. One or two bring luck.
- Two blackbirds sitting together bring good luck.
- If you see a duck fly, your relationships will be stable.
- A gull means you may soon travel, and a business trip will be successful.

45

Swing Along With Me

An easy type of divination to perform is *pendulum reading.* You can ask a "yes" or "no" question, then let the pendulum give you the answer by the direction of its swing.

Pendulum Reading

You'll Need
- a pendant or heavy ring
- a string about 45 cm (18 in.) long
- a pen and small sticky notes

1. To make a pendulum, loop the string through the ring or pendant. Tie the two ends of the string together.

2. Tune your pendulum by asking it a "yes" or "no" question to which you already know the answer. Example: "Is my name Cinderella?"

3. Over a tabletop, hold the pendulum at shoulder height. Relax your body and allow the pendulum to swing freely. In a few moments, you should see the pendulum begin to move in a clear direction. You now know that this swing direction means "no."

4. Mark one of your sticky notes with no, add the swing direction line and stick it to the table.

5. Do steps 2–4 with a "yes" question.

6. Repeat the tuning process several times to make sure you are reading your pendulum's swings correctly.

7. You may have to ask a series of questions to find the answer you want. For example, if you want to know if a trip is in your future, you might start with, "Will I travel anywhere on holiday?" If the answer is "yes," you can begin to narrow down the destination: "Will I travel to somewhere in Europe? Asia? North America?" etc.

8. Re-tune the pendulum each time the user changes.

Think About It!

Traditionally, many Mediterranean people have used pendulums to predict the sex of an unborn child. A threaded needle is the pendulum. It is held over the pregnant woman's stomach. If the swing is circular, the baby should be a girl. If the swing is in a line, the baby is believed to be a boy. As there are only two choices (boy or girl), you know you'd have a 50/50 chance of being correct with this technique.

Muscle Power

No one knows whether pendulums can really divine the future, but they do swing in definite patterns. Why? One possibility is that the diviner is unintentionally using her muscles to control the pendulum's swing. This is called the *Idiomotor Effect* and the results can be dramatic. During the 1800s, *table tapping* was popular. Participants would sit at a table with their fingertips resting on the surface. After a while, the table would seem to move on its own, turning and tilting off the floor. A scientific study showed that participants were actually causing this by moving their hands on the table, but they had no idea they were causing the table tapping themselves!

Scrying for Answers

Some divination techniques, called *scrying*, aid fortune-tellers in seeing images. Mirrors and bowls of water are popular scrying tools. So are crystal balls.

The fortune-teller looks into the ball, relaxing deeply in order to induce a trance. In this state, just like when you are beginning to fall asleep, images spontaneously rise in the mind. The fortune-teller may see the images in the depths of the crystal ball, or just in the imagination. If he sees a crown, for example, he reports his vision to the client. He then might add an interpretation: "You have powerful leadership abilities."

Mirror, Mirror, on the Wall

The wicked queen in the story *Snow White* was actually scrying when she asked her magic mirror, "Who is the fairest of them all?"

Tea Leaf Reading

You can experiment with scrying by trying another ancient art, tea leaf reading.

You'll Need
- a shallow bowl or teacup with sloping sides
- a pot of tea made from loose tea leaves (not in tea bags)
- saucer or plate

1. Pour the tea into the cup. A few leaves will swirl in the cup and eventually sink to the bottom.

2. Drink the tea, leaving a little bit in the bottom of the cup with the leaves.

3. Swirl the liquid in the cup, and then quickly turn the teacup over onto the saucer. Many of the tea leaves will cling to the sides of the cup.

4. Look at the tea leaves in the cup. Allow your mind to relax.

5. Use your imagination to describe what you see in the shapes made by the tea leaves.

What Do You **Think?**

Through the ages, people have attempted to trick time and peek into the future. You have tried a few of the many techniques designed to help divination, and you have explored how scientists test for precognition. Have you decided whether it's real or not? Want more to think about? The next chapter may move you closer to a decision!

Psychokinesis

When most people use the phrase "mind over matter," they mean that if they put their mind to something and really try hard, they can overcome obstacles. Psychics use it to mean something completely different. *Psychokinesis* (*PK*) is the ability to move or affect objects with the powers of the mind. Psychics who claim to have this skill say they can bend spoons, move objects, or change the course of events simply by willing it to happen.

Most scientists are very doubtful that PK exists. Newton's Laws of Motion say that there must be energy at work to cause motion or change. For example, your kick sends a soccer ball across a field—the energy goes from your foot to the ball. Without the kick, the ball would just stay put. Similarly, the energy from electricity powers up lights and computers. Without that energy, we'd be left in the dark.

Where is the energy in "mind over matter?" No one knows. But things just don't move by themselves. A psychic who states he can move objects with his mind is making a pretty far-fetched claim. A scientist would respond the same way that you do when someone tells you something unbelievable: "Yeah, right!"

Extraordinary claims require extraordinary proof. If someone says they can bend spoons with brainwaves, they're going to have to prove it. Their test results will have to be superb, their data beyond question. In short, people cannot just brag about their "supernatural" abilities and expect people to be amazed. The proof is in the pudding. If the proof is a spoon—and the spoon is bending— well, seeing may be believing!

When you consider it, nothing is absolutely impossible, including PK. Perhaps we just don't have measuring devices accurate enough to see the forces at work. Maybe we are looking in the wrong places. Keeping an open mind is important. Think of all those wise men who once insisted the Earth was flat.

Think About It!

The scientific process has its limits. For example, experimentation can only prove that a force or a phenomenon *does* exist. It cannot prove that it *doesn't*. The best scientists can do is say, "We have not yet proved the existence of PK at this time."

PK and the Power of Suggestion

Many stage magicians rely on the power of suggestion to perform their effects. The power of suggestion is so strong that it can alter people's behavior when they are under hypnosis. You often yawn when you see or read about someone else yawning. (Are you yawning now?) It can also have more subtle effects. For example, you might believe you saw someone move objects magically with their mind simply because you were expecting to. Try suggesting something to a friend, and see just how powerful you are.

Power of Suggestion Challenge

You'll Need
• a friend

1. Invite your friend into your bedroom.

2. Tell your friend that you spilled some itching powder on the bed. You have washed everything, but sometimes when you sit on your bed, you still get itchy.

3. Wait a moment or two, and then change the subject.

4. Scratch a little.

5. Watch closely. Does your friend begin to scratch too?

The Geller Effect

Uri Geller came to fame in the 1960s. He was a performer who appeared regularly on television with an astonishing act that involved bending spoons and causing watches to stop without touching them. In short, he was a PK pro.

Scientists, along with the general public, wanted to know if Geller truly was using solely his mind to perform his tricks, or if he was a phony. To find out, researchers at the Stanford Research Institute in California invited him to come to their lab and have his abilities scientifically tested. Geller passed all of his lab tests with flying colors. The researchers were so impressed that they dubbed psychokinesis the *Geller Effect.*

Many stage magicians, however, scoffed at Geller. They claimed that the tricks he did were ones anyone could do—with a little know-how. They thought he relied on the power of suggestion and on old-fashioned sleight of hand. A magician named the Amazing Randi was Geller's biggest critic. He said that Geller's feats were "the kind that used to be on the back of cereal boxes when I was a kid." Was Geller for real? More than 30 years later, people still argue about him. A challenge or two may help you decide.

Think About It!

In Haiti, people traditionally practiced *voodoo,* a religion that was based in ancient African rituals. Voodoo sorcerers sometimes placed a curse on an enemy. The curse would turn him into a *zombie,* or the "living dead." Within a few days, the person would stop eating and sleeping. He would no longer recognize friends or enemies. In fact, there have been many documented cases in which the victims died.

No one knows for sure how voodoo curses worked. Some think it was an example of the power of suggestion: once cursed, the victim's belief in the curse made it come true! Others think this may have been PK at work. Still others believe poison was involved.

Spoon Bender Bash

Can you bend spoons with your mind? Host a spoon-bending party to try it out. Whether or not you succeed, you'll have a great time trying.

You'll Need
- about 12 friends
- old spoons that you have permission to bend (You might want to buy these at a garage sale or flea market.)

1. Create an atmosphere of excitement and fun for your party. Lots of laughter and a sense of humor will help your experiment go well.

2. Have your guests choose a utensil. Have them ask it, "Will you bend for me?" If they don't think the utensil will bend, have them choose another one.

3. Once you select your spoon, immediately hold it upright in front of you and shout, "Bend! Bend!" This is what Uri Geller did.

4. Next, rub the spoon gently between two fingers, back and forth along the neck. It may bend without your using any force at all.

Scientific Proof

Most scientists think PK is pretty unconvincing. Nevertheless, there is evidence that indicates PK may exist! One experiment showed that human thought could influence computers. The experiment involved simple computers called random number generators. The test showed that a person concentrating on a particular number could make this number appear more often than chance would predict. The effect was slight, but real and measurable.

Think About It!

People who believe in Psi are more likely to have Psi experiences. If you believe your spoon will bend, it is more likely to cooperate!

PK Dice Challenge

You'll Need

- one regular die
- score sheet and pencil or pen
- a shaker cup

1 Choose a number from one to six. Concentrate on it. Try to roll this number as often as possible during the experiment.

2 Using the shaker cup, roll the die 100 times.

3 Record the results for each roll.

4 Repeat the series of 100 rolls three times. At the end of the three series, total up the times you rolled your number. Compare your results to the score below.

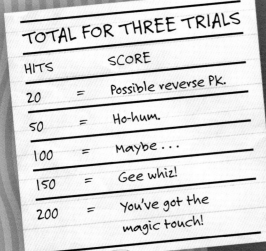

TOTAL FOR THREE TRIALS		
HITS		SCORE
20	=	Possible reverse PK.
50	=	Ho-hum.
100	=	Maybe . . .
150	=	Gee whiz!
200	=	You've got the magic touch!

Dice and the Laws of Probability

When you tried the dice challenge, you had a one in six chance of rolling a six. What about if you rolled two dice at a time? Would you still have a one out of six chance of rolling that six?

Nope. According to the laws of probability, with two dice, there are 36 possible combinations that you can roll. There are only five ways to roll a six out of those 36. That's *less* than a one in six chance. There is even a worse chance of rolling a two. Odds are that you will roll a seven more often than any other combination. Is seeing believing? Try the Double Dice Challenge on the next page!

Double Dice Challenge

You'll Need

- a pair of dice
- score sheet and pencil or pen
- a shaker cup

1 Roll the dice.

2 Record the results of the roll on your score sheet.

3 Repeat 100 times.

4 Add up the number of times you rolled each possible number: 2, 3, etc.

5 Which number did you roll most often? Which did you roll least often? Compare your results to those shown below. According to the laws of probability, in a hundred rolls of two dice, you would roll a:

2	fewer than 3 times
3	fewer than 6 times
4	fewer than 9 times
5	fewer than 11 times
6	fewer than 14 times
7	about 17 times
8	fewer than 14 times
9	fewer than 11 times
10	fewer than 9 times
11	fewer than 6 times
12	fewer than 3 times

If your numbers weren't similar to these results, read on for a possible explanation.

When Bigger Is Better

Let's say you roll the dice ten times. The laws of probability say that on each roll, you are more likely to roll a seven than a two, right? So what would you think if you rolled a two ten times in a row? A lot of people would think something pretty weird was going on—maybe even something psychic. But mathematicians know that the weirdness is just an illusion. It even has a name: the *clustering illusion.*

Over the long run, you will roll more sevens in total than twos. But you have to roll lots and lots and lots of times for this to happen. In a shorter series of rolls, there's just not enough data to give clear results. Ten is not enough. Even 100 is not really enough. Ten thousand trials is more like what you'd need to see the effects of probability accurately.

Coin Toss Conundrum

Flip a coin 20 times. How likely do you think it is to get four heads in a row? The laws of chance say you'll get four heads in a row 50% of the time! Surprised? Try it yourself and see!

Are They Hot? Guess Not!

You can see the clustering illusion at work in major league sports. Fans, players, and coaches alike believe that basketball players, hockey players, baseball players, and other athletes have "hot" or "cold streaks." They think that during a short period of time, individuals sometimes score much better or worse than probability would suggest. Often they think it's something to do with the athlete and how he feels, what he's doing differently, or how hard he's trying.

Not a chance, say the scientists. A study of the Philadelphia 76ers showed that during the 1980–81 season, the number of baskets scored in a row was exactly as predicted by chance, whether the player was "hot" or "cold."

A Healthy Dose of PK?

Scientific studies have shown that PK may be able to help heal illness. In a controlled experiment with AIDS patients, published in *The Western Journal of Medicine*, psychic healers were asked to concentrate on and pray for certain patients in an effort to improve their health. The patients were not told about the experiment. The patients who were prayed for did significantly better than the other patients in the control group who were not prayed for.

Another, larger study conducted on heart patients showed that the patients who were prayed for had fewer complications, needed fewer antibiotics, and required less mechanical breathing assistance than heart patients who did not receive long-distance thought waves.

In the case of voodoo, the negative power of bad thoughts could be put down to a person knowing about a zombie curse, and being so afraid that the power of suggestion made the victim fall ill. But in these cases the patients were strangers, and did not know about the positive thoughts being sent their way. Some scientists think PK may be at the root of the explanation. People with deep religious beliefs might simply say that the power of prayer is at work. What do you say?

Think About It!

Can thought waves be so strong that they can actually transform into some kind of physical force?

Sneaky PK

Many PK effects can be performed by stage magicians using old-fashioned sleight of hand. Try these examples from the professional magician's bag of tricks.

Spoon-Bending
Mind Bender

If you didn't succeed in bending a spoon at your party, you can always fake it. Some critics of Uri Geller say this is the method he used. If you decide to try it, practice hard first. Only really good magicians can pull it off!

You'll Need
- a cheap, easily bent metal spoon
- an audience

1 You will simply bend the spoon using good old muscle power. The trick is to do it without being noticed by your audience. If people want to believe it is PK at work, they will see PK at work. Most people will be skeptical at first—you'll really have to be convincing!

2 Grip the spoon at the neck (the thinnest part) using thumb and forefinger. Your little finger should be placed on the edge of the handle.

3 Using the other hand, grasp the bowl of the spoon between your thumb and forefinger.

4 Press and bend the spoon backward, pulling the bowl down.

Ye Olde
Dancing Straw Trick

Convince your friends that you are using PK to make a straw move on the tabletop.

You'll Need
- a plastic straw

1 Explain to your audience that you will control the motion of the straw using PK.

2 Place the straw on the table.

3 Secretly and quietly take a deep breath and hold it.

4 Wave your hand over the straw as if to magically move it. Lower your face close to the straw and appear to be concentrating hard on it.

5 Very gently, blow through your nostrils and move the straw. You will have to practice doing this ahead of time to get the blowing just right: your audience must not see or hear your blowing.

6 Do not repeat this trick because it is so simple and obvious that someone is bound to catch on once the element of surprise is gone.

Think About It!

You might say that trickery goes hand-in-hand with PK. But at the same time, not everything about PK can be proven to be a trick. What do you think? Is PK the real deal, or really ridiculous?

Ye Olde Levitating
Matchbox Trick

With some practice you can make this work successfully. But it is most effective if not repeated. You only have the element of surprise on your side once.

You'll Need
• a cardboard matchbox, matches removed

1. Open the little drawer in the matchbox. Hold the matchbox in your hand. Your hand should be relaxed and slightly cupped. The drawer should be open, and pointing toward your thumb.

2. Close the drawer carefully, pinching some of the skin at the base of your thumb with the drawer.

3. Explain to your audience that you will make the matchbox magically levitate. Your audience must all be in front of you.

4. Make some spooky sounds and wave your free hand over the matchbox. Make levitating motions.

5. Slowly straighten out the hand that is holding the matchbox. The box will appear to rise by itself!

6. Relax your hand, closing the little drawer at the same time. Allow your audience to examine the matchbox and try the trick on their own.

Nothing Is Certain
and
That's for Certain

In this book, you have explored a tiny corner of the world of ESP. You have seen how people the world over and through the ages have believed in its power. Entire civilizations rose and fell on the words of prophets and seers. Legends and literature from North America to Asia feature stories of the unexplained or tell about psychic dreams.

ESP is not just ancient history or superstition. More than half of the people in the world today have had some kind of psychic experience. Interest in divining methods such as tarot cards and crystals, horoscopes and pendulums, is at an all-time high.

You could easily make a case that psychic ability is a universal human trait. On the other hand, you have learned that ESP is hard to prove and often faked. People can be fooled into seeing a psychic event where none exists by the power of suggestion, the Law of Truly Large Numbers, or a plain old trick.

¿

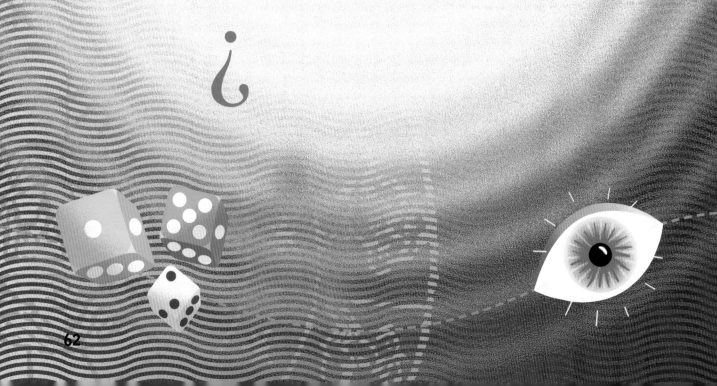

What Do You Think?

After examining the evidence and performing your own challenges, what is your opinion? Do you think ESP is likely or unlikely? What would it take to convince you either way? Perhaps you will be the researcher who some day proves that ESP is real. Or maybe it will be your experiment that debunks the theory once and for all. No one knows for sure what fate has in store for us. But one thing is certain: whatever your future holds, it will be up to you to make it happen.

Index